AF797498

Behind The Mask
INVISIBLE PAIN

A Path To Holistic Healing

ANTOINETTE MICHELLE TERRY

Behind The Mask-Invisible Pain

Copyright © 2020 by Antoinette Michelle Terry

All rights reserved. No part of this book may be reproduced or transmitted in any form or by any means without written permission from the author.

ISBN (**978-0-578-71662-6**)

Printed in the USA by Antoinette Michelle Terry

CONTENTS

Dedication

I am dedicating this book to all of my fellow women and men who suffer from Rheumatoid Arthritis, Fibromyalgia, Lupus, and other chronic autoimmune painful diseases. I love you all, and I pray for us every day. I want to give a special shout out to my fellow warriors of my Facebook Page RA and Fibromyalgia-Behind The Mask Invisible Pain Support Group. I come to rely on the strength I draw from speaking with some of you every day. It makes a world of difference and reassures you that you are not alone and that someone out there understands your struggle completely.

Most of our close family and friends do not understand the complete picture because most of what we feel is invisible. I want to thank each one of you for your prayers and encouraging words you have given me. I pray that I have been a blessing to you, as well. Thank you all for joining and recognizing with me the need to create a safe and loving environment for us who struggle with these diseases to vent and just be us.

Queen of Trauma Drama

Acknowledgements

I would like to acknowledge Anthony Williams of Uncovered Story Publishing for encouraging me to move forward with publishing this book. He gave me tools and alternative methods to use which made it easier to get my thoughts on paper. I am grateful for all the help and attention he gave me along this journey of becoming an author.

Foreword

This is a powerful story of the physical and emotional burdens of living with severe chronic pain. In this instance, the cause was rheumatoid arthritis. But the story applies to any chronic pain syndrome. Reading this account will help patients with chronic pain, their families, close friends, and healthcare professionals. Ms. Terry describes the fulminate onset and incapacitating course of her disease. She explores how some of her family, close friends, and even healthcare professionals cast doubt on the reality of her pain when externally visible signs of a source were minimal or "invisible." She ultimately finds hope and help through her strong religious faith and support groups.

Several years ago, when she was early in her illness, I met Ms. Terry. She was hospitalized in a teaching hospital. I was not involved in her care but met her in a teaching session. A group of two medical students, three postgraduate physician trainees, a librarian (who helped access information for patients and health care professionals), and I gathered at her bedside for about 40 minutes. After a brief moment of introduction and interaction, it was clear she had a powerful lesson for healthcare professionals. She became the "professor." In the most compelling terms, she taught us all how to be better physicians: know your patient well, listen carefully and examine with sensitivity without assuming a joint did not hurt because it was not obviously inflamed. She taught us the importance of empathy, compassion, and continued continuity as we tried to help a patient through a continuing health nightmare. The lesson she gave us that day was so poignant that I asked her to consider writing a short play that might tell the story of a patient with "invisible pain" to use in our education program. Within a few weeks, two scripts arrived. We read these in a large classroom session. All were moved by the compelling story of suffering often without acknowledgment from others or empathy from physicians. She taught us well.

Now she has created this book, which is certain to provide comfort and insight to those suffering with chronic invisible pain and their families. While the book focuses on women, it has applicability to all. For healthcare professionals, it is a salient and moving accounting of how we can improve as healthcare providers by knowing our patients carefully and diligently guiding them through their medical nightmare and doing so with empathy and compassion.

John Burton, MD
Professor of Medicine Emeritus
The Johns Hopkins University School of Medicine

Introduction

Pain that is indescribable that's all I can say. Even after suffering from RA for at least six years, I still cannot describe the pain. It feels so intense that you feel like you are dying and at times. The people around you look at you and can't see your pain or the degree of it and just don't understand. We are conditioned to look for tangible things. Most people believe if they can't see it, feel it, touch it, hear it, or see evidence of it, then it doesn't exist. I think most people believe that we do have a disease, the level of our struggle, and how we are forced to deal with it because they have a hard time believing?

Just get up, and you'll feel better? How many times have you heard this? You lie there thinking to yourself, if only they knew how exhausted I feel right now. I can't even lift my arms to brush my teeth or comb my hair. You wish that they would just leave you alone.

My prayer is that someone who reads this book receives divine revelation into the depth of the struggle that someone they may know who has one of these chronic conditions goes through and can support them without judgment. And that someone who is suffering receives divine peace, comfort, healing, and love from our Savior, the Lord Jesus Christ.

"Come unto to me, all that labor and are heavy laden, and I will give you rest. Take my yoke upon you and learn of me, for I am meek and lowly in heart, and you will find rest for your souls. For my yoke is easy and my burdens are light"

Matthew 11:28-30

I Remember the Day

I remember the day as if it just happened today. The first time I felt the pain of Rheumatoid Arthritis at its fullest fiery. Not even knowing at the time that was what I was feeling, I woke up thinking I was dying. I had just had major surgery seven days earlier. I had gotten a partial hysterectomy. I actually did well with the surgery. I came home two days after the surgery because the doctors were impressed with how well I was doing, and I was also. Within twenty-four hours, I was taking a shower. I felt great. I was in a little pain, of course, but I was feeling so good that I decided that I didn't need the strong pain medicine anymore. I figured I'd just switch to Tylenol or Advil.

The Day I Yelled "HELP!"

On the seventh day, all hell broke loose. My eyes were closed, and I remember not wanting to open them, because I didn't understand why my body felt the way it did. I didn't know what was going on, and I didn't know what I was going to open my eyes to find. When I opened my eyes, I looked at my body, and it didn't look any different. I screamed with the loudest scream. I think I've ever yelled, "HELP." At one moment, my husband and my two sons ran into my bedroom. I said, "something's wrong with me. I can't move. It hurts so much. Oh, my God, help me." I remember my youngest boy Troy just started crying. My husband asked me where does it hurt, and I told him everywhere. My oldest son, Derek, said, "I need to call 911." My husband told him not to and insisted on taking me to the hospital himself.

I remember him carrying me in the car. I could not walk at all—every movement I made riddle my body with excruciating pain. I thought I was going to lose my mind. I thought to myself, this is it. I must be dying. My husband parked the car outside the ER and went in to get a wheelchair. A nurse came out to help him, and when she saw my condition, she took me straight to the back.

I was screaming and crying, so loud tears were pouring down my face. My vital signs were off the charts. I couldn't catch my breath. I knew I was now also having a full-blown panic attack on top of everything else. They started an IV and took some blood, and the doctor came in to talk to me. After asking me what seemed like a thousand questions, he finally gave me some morphine for pain. It barely touched it. Then he gave me some Dilaudid by injection.

Finally, the pain eased up a bit. It didn't go away, but it wasn't as intense. My blood work came back, and the doctor said that my body's inflammation levels were severe enough to cause false positives on lupus tests. I began to panic. He reassured me that he didn't think I had lupus. He said that he was going to start me on a high dose of steroids for the inflammation, give me a script for some pain medication, and that I needed to see a rheumatoid specialist within a couple of days. He referred me to a doctor at the hospital, and there started my journey with RA.

The Uncertainty After The First Office Visit

I had no idea what to expect on this visit. I knew of no one at that time in my family who had RA so no one could tell me anything. I searched on Google for RA, and of course, that scared the crap out of me. So the doctor comes in the room, and I'm still not feeling too good. He reaches out to shake my hand. I tell him I can't because my hands hurt. He says, “okay." He asked me questions, and I answered them the best I could. He checks the blood work from the Emergency Room visit and confirms that my inflammation levels were extremely high. He said between the bloodwork and my physical symptoms, I had a high RA factor number and that he was diagnosing me with severe RA. I said, "Okay, what does that mean?"

He stated that my RA factor number was 42, which is severe. He told me that RA was an autoimmune disease and gave me a pamphlet. He started me on a drug called Methotrexate at the minimum dose. He ordered bloodwork to do some more extensive tests and told me to wean off of the steroids. He wanted to see me back in six weeks when the steroids were complete.

So What Do You Do? Now!

I remember making my next appointment looking at my mother with a puzzled look on my face. She asked, “So what do you do, Toni?” I said, "I guess I read this pamphlet. I don't know." I felt more confused about my condition with a diagnosis than before I came in for the appointment. I know thousands of women all over the world who left their first office visit to the doctor were just as confused as I was. I was thinking to myself that I just saw a specialist in the field, yet he didn't really tell me anything special about it, other than you have it.

Everyone around you wants to know more about what's going on with you and what they can do to help you. They're asking you the same questions you need answers. That begins our inability to explain our disease to our family and friends. They're uncomfortable because we're uncomfortable. So everyone tries to be supportive by encouraging you to try to go back to the way you were before. Get back to your daily routines is what they say, not understand that your daily routines are not so routine anymore. You lack energy, strength, and you're in pain. Although it may be a little better, it’s still present. I remember getting naked and sitting in front of the mirror in my bedroom, staring at my body and trying to see what I was feeling, but I couldn't. My body looked the same as it did before. Yet from my neck down to my toes, I felt pain. How could I explain that? I didn't understand it.

The truth is, I still don't understand fully. I know that when I try to explain how I feel to the doctors, they look at me like they haven't got a clue about how I feel, and they just don't understand. I've grown to learn unless you suffer with it, you will never fully understand, and that goes for everyone, including the doctors.

The Medication Journey

"No weapon formed against me shall prosper."

Isaiah 54:17

I began to quote this scripture every single day when my journey of different medications started. You have your steroids, Methotrexate, biologic pills, biologic injections, biologic infusions, and don't forget chemical chemo infusions. If it's not the cost of the medications that get you, then it's the horrible and downright nasty side effects. Although most of the time, it's both of those things. The side effects are so brutal at times, nausea, vomiting, diarrhea, stomach pains, headaches, irritability, mood swings, hot flashes, sweating, and dry mouth, to name a few. And believe it or not more pain. So much so that you contemplate whether you should just try to take the pain. I doubt if anyone decides to do that, though.

Up and Down With Medications

I started to look at the medications as weapons that were not fighting for me but against me. My insurance company wanted me to try one medication before they would approve the one the doctor wanted to prescribe. So I felt like that process kept me in pain for a few months to see if they could save money for a few months. The doctor already knew the medication they wanted me to try wouldn't work. The entire time I went through the different medications, I was placed on and off steroids. I call it the "steroid shuffle." I go up, and then I go down. I go all the way off and then back around. I'm doing the "steroid shuffle." That's the little chant I made up. I used to sing this song to different tunes when I went to the doctor, and his only solution was to put me back on steroids.

Over the last six years, I have gained and lost over 125 plus pounds. My weight goes up and down like a roller coaster. It seems like a never-ending cycle that I'm to this day still on. So let's analyze this and break it down real good. Most of us are in severe pain in every joint, taking meds that cause horrible side effects both physically and emotionally, feeling hopeless, depressed, exhausted, and can barely walk or do daily functions. And you wonder why you are withdrawn, irritable, and just want to be left alone.

Sometimes people wonder why we are not at the family functions. We are at home wishing we were there with you. Our hearts and minds want to be there, but our bodies aren't cooperating that day. I used to try and make everything and do everything my family and friends wanted me to do. I would be at a function in severe pain, or I would pay for it afterward by having severe pain.

Now I just say a polite no, sorry, I can't, or sorry I won't be able to make it. I've realized that things will go on without me, and I don't need to cause myself any unnecessary pain or stress. Now, for once in a lifetime events like weddings, for example, I may try to press my way. Either way, I no longer feel guilty and nor should you.

Surviving Broken Relationships

The truth of the matter is these chronic pain illnesses can interfere with and break up the strongest relationships. Every spouse, partner, friend, and other family members will start off being supportive. But unfortunately, as you continue to battle with the illness, it takes its toll on your relationships. Let's go back to Chapter One - I Remember The Day and reflect on how I spoke about my now ex-husband. He started loving, concerned, and very helpful. He stayed that way for at least two years. As life continued to throw its blows, it became evident that he was sick and tired of me being sick and tired.

I Lost My Job and Everything Changed

I lost my job unfairly due to my illness. So he became the primary breadwinner, and everything started changing. He complained more and more and helped me less and less. There were days he came home, and he didn't even speak to me because I had been in bed all day sick. We stopped sleeping in the same bed together at night because I was always in pain, and every time he would move in the bed, I would moan in pain. Before we knew it, we were living like roommates. We grew further and further apart, and I resented him for not sticking in there for the better and worse. Some days he was just outright mean to me.

I thank God for my two sons. They were my saving grace and still are to this day. I don't know what I would do without them. After several attempts at marriage counseling and spiritual guidance, I finally asked my husband for a divorce. The stress of being in an unhealthy and unhappy marriage began to have adverse effects on my health. When I get the chance to talk to young women who have these illnesses who are upset because their boyfriend left them or wants to leave them, I have this advice for them, let them go. This person is already showing you that they are not in it for the long haul and that trying to hold on only adversely affects you and your illness. Forget what you had, because they forgot as well.

This disease changes you and the people closest to your lives. Especially how you manage your day-to-day. Some people cannot handle change. For us who battle with these illnesses, we have no choice. When it gets hard, and the people around me don't understand, my faith keeps me going.

"I can do all things through Christ who gives me strength."

Philippians 4:13

This is one of my favorite scriptures because it reminds me that my strength is in Jesus. When everyone seems to have failed me, when it seems like I can't make it another day, and I just want to give up, it reminds me that He is there to strengthen me, and I press on. I remember one night, the pain was so intense, and no matter what I did, it would not go away. The pain medicine didn't work. I tried ice and heat, and nothing would work. So I laid in my bed crying and just started calling Jesus' name. All I kept saying while I was crying was Jesus, Jesus, Jesus, over and over again. I don't know how long I did it. I don't remember falling asleep. But I woke up several hours later well-rested, and my pain had decreased significantly.

Sometimes it may seem like you're all alone. It doesn't matter if no one understands because if they understood, they still couldn't help you. That's when you turn to Jesus. Our present help in the time of trouble. We are never alone. He is always with us. I gave Jesus the biggest hallelujah praise when I woke up, and my son Derek ran into my room and said, "What happened?" I jumped off the bed and showed him that I could move Derek said, "hallelujah." Then he gave me the biggest hug.

Facing The Fear Behind The Mask

There are so many types of fear that can be associated with these types of illnesses. You have a fear of the unknown. Why do I have it? What caused me to get it? How long will I be in pain? Will, any of the medications work? Will I become crippled? Can I have children? Will they get it? The list goes on and on and on. Imagine yourself being afraid to go to sleep at night for fear that when you open your eyes the next morning, your body will be riddled with crippling pain. I lived in that exact fear for the entire first year of my illness.

Living In Fear and Pain

I was so afraid of feeling the pain level I felt the first time that I would stay up all night. No matter how hard I tried to go to sleep, I could never go until it was morning, and I could barely hold my eyes open. I didn't know at the time it was fear. Looking back on it now, I think I was thinking if I made it to the morning, without the pain increasing, it was safe for me to go to sleep. This made my already exhausted body even more tired. I never shared it with anyone that I was living like this every night. It did not help my condition at all. I didn't realize I was living in fear until my Bishop preached a sermon on the spirit of fear.

"For God didn't give us a spirit of fear but of power, and of love and a sound mind."

2 Timothy 1:7

He spoke about fear being a spirit that can attach itself to you when you are vulnerable. That attack is in the mind. It's usually an exaggerated thought about something you cannot control. But one thing's for sure it's not from God. The sermon hit me like a ton of bricks. I thought to myself how irrational I had been thinking I could control the pain by staying up. It's funny to me now, but it wasn't then. My breakthrough didn't come right then but later in the service when the Jubilee choir began to sing the hymn - Many Things About Tomorrow.

When I heard the chorus, sing "Many Things About Tomorrow," I don't seem to understand, but I know who holds the future, and I know who holds my hand. It increased my faith to know that even though I might not know how I'm going to feel tomorrow or the next day or the next day, God knows all things. And he promised that he would not put more on me than I could bear. So I might have to feel some pain, but it is not unto death, even though it feels like it. I feel the desire to continue to move, continue to press on, and not allow fear to be my driving force. Am I going to be cripple? Well, I have a debilitating disease, but I could get hit by a car and become crippled. I could fall down the steps and become crippled; it's no different than that.

I have to keep trusting in God and taking my medications. Keep moving and not just lay around in the bed. I had to try to do things, especially on a good day. A good day for me is pain under a level four. I feel that the worst thing you can do with these diseases is sitting still all the time. You know, we have to press our way because when we sit still, fear sets in. We don't live our lives in fear. We didn't live our lives in fear before this disease. We went outside every day after we would hear about gun shootings, or we would hear about robberies, etc. But our faith kept us going every day to the places that we wanted to go and doing the things we wanted to do, and we have to keep that same mindset with this disease.

There are good and bad days and in-between days, and unless I was totally crippled with pain, I would move around even if it was just in my home. I refuse to live my life in fear because God did not give me that spirit. So I refuse to live that way. I pray that you refuse to live your life in fear, as well.

The Benefits Of Accepting The Diagnosis

I finally got to a point where accepting my diagnosis became a very important part of my emotional health. It allowed me to go through the grieving process. Believe it or not, there is a grieving process that goes along with having these chronic diseases. The disease is not going to go away. You can go into remission, but you can still have symptoms. You will live for the rest of your life with it. I had to face that. So accepting the diagnosis allowed me to grieve.

Stepping Through The Grieving Process

I mean, by grieve, I had to let go of the person I used to be. It's not that the person that I am now is worse than the person that I used to be. She's just different. Believe it or not, going through this extreme excruciating pain has changed you. No, you're not able to do all the things that you used to do, and some days you can't even take a shower because you're so exhausted. Trying to be who you used to is a struggle, and if you stay at that place of "struggle," it can cause you to become depressed and upset that you're not who you used to be. But if you accept your diagnosis and go through the grieving process, you'll learn to love who you are now, even though you can't do some of the things you used to. I did. I learn to embrace the new me realizing that

I'm still fabulous, and so are you.

Accepting the diagnosis, and the changes, helps you to continue to go on with your life. Because it doesn't make you worse, it doesn't make you bad. It doesn't make you anything but different from who you used to be. I can say about me going through this pain, it not only produced some negativity and some anger for a while about having to deal with this, but it produced some positive characteristics in me as well. I became very empathetic and sympathetic to other people that I may not have been in the past. I don't want to say I was ever a bad person. However, when I look back, I did have a different perspective.

I know that I used to believe that everybody that was addicted to drugs was in that state because they wanted to be. That they just wanted to party and have what they considered to be a good time. And that was how they became addicted to drugs. I no longer see it that way only. One day I was in my car, and my mom was driving because I was in pain, we passed a street corner in Baltimore, MD, where there is a methadone clinic. So right outside of the clinic, right on that corner, there's always people hanging out there who go to the methadone clinic. Some of them are getting high and drinking. In the past, I would be a little judgmental with my thoughts, but this time I had an epiphany. I wondered how many of them have turned to street drugs and alcohol to self-medicate from diseases because with no medical insurance to see a health care professional, so they self-medicate for the pain.

Although I had medical insurance on my job, when I first was diagnosed with this disease, I still struggled because the medicine that they wanted to give me had copays sometimes in the thousands of dollars. I was working, so it made me think, okay, if I was not working, and on social services, or not on any type of assistance, and I started getting this type of pain, I may have started taking over counter medicines. However, I know now that they eventually stop working. You never know a person's backstory as to why they are the way they are. I had gained a different perspective. I've talked to several other people who have these diseases, and most have had some kind of epiphany.

Living Life with Empathy

What it does is it opens your mind to be empathetic for people. Not just for people who suffer from physical pain but emotional pain as well. These diseases take you through both. You have physical and emotional pain, which causes you to be more concerned about others than you might have been in the past. And yes, I wish I would have been that way before the diseases, but after being diagnosed with RA and Fibromyalgia, accepting my diagnosis and going through the things that I've been through has caused me to look at people in their situations differently. I feel like I'm not the same person, but I'm a better person in many ways.

So, accepting your diagnosis and going through the grieving

process, allowing yourself to change, allowing your thoughts to change, letting how you deal with things to change will toughen you up. Also, it will soften you up and cause you to be empathetic towards other people. So yes, you are different than you were. Stop and look at yourself, look at how you think, and look at what you're doing now that you may not have been doing before. You may be volunteering now, or you may be doing things that you didn't do before because you were working, and you didn't have the time. Positively look at your life even though you have one or more of these diseases. It first starts with you accepting the diagnosis.

How I Took Control of My Health Care

It became so apparent to me around the second year after being diagnosed with RA, that I needed to get involved in my health care. I needed to take control of my health care. In the beginning, I was so overwhelmed with the diagnosis and the pain. The doctors were unable to give me detailed information. I was being put on medications and provided information about the side effects only. I didn't understand what the medication did or how it was going to work in my body.

At two years, I was just tired, and I didn't want to fully rely on the doctors anymore. I thought to myself, this is my body, and I need to be involved. Mentally I needed to be involved with what was happening with me. So, what I started to do was research. I would research not only the medication I was on but also all the medications for the treatment of RA. My fellow warriors, we have a chronic disease, and it's never going to go away. We can go into remission; however, even in remission, we can have flare-ups. It's different for each one of us. Researching the disease and the medication helped me play a significant role in my health care.

Document Your Way To A Healthier Life

Another thing that I did was start to document how I felt

every day in a daily journal. I would answer these questions every day:

- What is my pain level?
- What was my activity?
- What did I eat or drink?
- What is my stress level?
- Was I stiff and how long did it last?

It may seem tedious, but I got used to documenting this critical information daily. It easily became a part of my daily routine. I would also document:

- What made the pain feel better or worse?
- Did I need to take pain medication?
- What I did the day before?
- What I did the night before?
- What did I eat when I got up in the morning?
- What was the weather like?

Documenting this information helped me get a clearer picture of:

- How my body was responding to medication?
- How my body was responding to my diet?
- How my body was responding to physical exertion and how my body felt with no physical exertion?

- Did the weather affect how I was feeling?

Learning The Patterns of Your Illness

I learned a lot about the patterns related to my illness. So much so, I was able to go in on my appointments and tell my doctor how I was feeling every day since my last visit. I could let the doctor know what days/weeks were good or bad.

. I was limited to only telling the doctor how I had been feeling for the last couple of days before the visit wasn't enough. Sometimes I would feel good for the few days before the office visit, but the three weeks prior, I had been in pain.

After I started collecting data on my health and taking control, I was able to give my doctor became very valuable to my health care.

The more information I was able to give my doctor, the more involved I became in my health care.

My doctor became more comfortable because he knew that I was taking control of my health care. He saw that I was investing in getting myself better or a least in a better situation. I was able to tell him right away when something didn't work. I was able to let him know when I needed some prednisone to help with flares. I was able to guide him in my care. I believe that I became more valuable to him in my care than he was to me. Yes, he could prescribe the medications; however, what and when he would prescribe a medication relied heavily on the information I was able to give him.

Taking these steps in my health care took away that feeling of hopelessness. I felt more in control and not so overwhelmed anymore. Learning my body and recognizing patterns helps me make more informed decisions about my diet and physical activity. I could really make a conscious choice on whether I will eat a particular food or do a specific activity because I knew the outcome from past experience. It's a little different for everyone, so you need to learn your body, but there is a method for the madness. Those first couples of years, I would have never believed that I could take control of my health care the way I am now.

I just thought everything was out of my control. I believed I had no control and very little to say regarding mt illness. That wasn't true for me, and it isn't true for you.

The more you can learn; about your body and your diet, your body and physical exertion, and when flare-ups happen and possible reasons, the more in control you feel.

Think about it, the doctor is only seeing you for 45 minutes every four to six weeks, but you're with yourself every day. So, every single day, love yourself by documenting your health and what's going on with you. And once you get that big picture, it will help you so much, both physically and mentally as well as it did me.

Having Faith Leads to Holistic Healing

Having faith is a very big part of my healing process. I don't know what I would have done if I did not have faith in God and my belief in Him as a Healer. I trust God, and I believe that by His stripes, we are healed. Hearing the word "chronic disease" and knowing that we will always have the disease can, at times, make us feel like the situation is hopeless. But in Christ Jesus, there is always hope.

I remember experiencing severe pain nights, and neither my ex-husband, my sons, or pain medication could ease my pain. Nothing could help. It didn't matter how much my husband, my sons, even my mother wanted to help me; there was nothing that they could do.

I would get permission to take a higher dose of pain medication to ease the pain, but it didn't work.

Then I'd called on the name of Jesus. I spoke about this in one of my earlier chapters. I'm never going to forget this night because nothing I tried would help. It was excruciating pain, and I felt like I was dying. I thought to myself, who could live through this pain. I found myself through faith, calling on the name of Jesus. I knew in my heart and my spirit that was where my help was going to come. There is none like Jesus. There is none like our Savior. Having a strong faith can and will get us through some really hard times. Not only regarding this disease but in everything in life as we struggle and go through trials and tribulations.

Now I know that being saved and being a Christian is someone who has made and allowed Jesus to be head of their life. I wasn't always this person. I asked Jesus to come into my life and save me at age sixteen, but I wasn't walking in God's will. I was walking on my own will. Over the years, as I experienced trials and tribulations, I have learned that God's will is the safest place for me. I have surrendered my life to Him completely. I now put my trust in God, which has increased my faith. Having a strong faith is important for Holistic Healing. We are made up of a body, a soul, and a spirit. Our health can fail and become diseased in all of these areas. We are all born into the disease of sin, which affects our soul and spirit. The world is blessed to have doctors, scientists, and researchers who have received wisdom from God on effective treatments, medications, therapies, and surgeries to aid in the healing of various diseases and illnesses of the body, which includes the mind. The soul and spirit, however, requires a supernatural experience outside of human capacity.

It is here at this point where I am compelled to ask you, the reader, a question. Have you accepted Jesus Christ into your life as your personal Savior? Jesus is the cure for our wounded souls. God has a plan of Salvation for our life.

The first step is to recognize all have sinned.

"For all have sinned and fall short of the glory of God"

Romans 3:23

Second, we must know the consequences of sin.

"For the wages of sin is death; but the gift of God is eternal life through Jesus Christ our Lord."

Romans 6:23

Third we must know that Christ died for us.

"But God demonstrates His own love toward us, in that, while we were yet sinners, Christ died for us."

Romans 5:8

The fourth step is to confess and believe.

"That if you confess with your mouth the
Lord Jesus and believe in your heart
that God has raised Him from the dead,
you will be saved."

Romans 10:9

And last is the results of Salvation.

"Therefore, being justified by faith, we have peace with God Through our Lord Jesus Christ"

Romans 5:1

If you do not know Jesus in the parting of your sins and your desire to give your life to Christ and ask Him to come into your life and save you, repeat this in your heart and with your mouth:

Lord, I know and confess that I am a sinner. I was born in sin and shaped inequity. I know that I am doing things that are not pleasing in your sight. I want you to know that I confess with my mouth that You are Lord and Savior. You were born of the Virgin Mary, and you walked this earth, healing the sick and raising the dead. You were nailed to a cross and died a crucifixion death for my sins. On the third day, God raised you from the dead with all power in your hands. I believe this with my whole heart. Lord, I repent of my sins and ask that you come into my life and save me. I want you Jesus to come into my life and make me whole. Would you come into my life today, Jesus?

I believe that if you repeated those words, and you met them, that Jesus is now living on the inside of you, and you are now saved. I pray that the Holy Spirit would lead you to a Bible-based church that will allow you to learn and to grow in God's grace.

Faith Is the Linkage to Holistic Healings

Faith is an essential part of Holistic Healing. It ties everything together, and the whole person is healed. Once Jesus comes into your life, and you're given a measure of the Holy Spirit, it will be the Holy Spirit that:

- encourages you
- comforts you
- lead and guide you
- strengthen you
- help you pray
- pray for you
- empowers you
- remind you that there is hope

It will be the Holy Spirit that will get you up and get you going even when you feel as though you can't because you feel weak. He is strong. My faith has bought me through some pretty hard times with this disease, and each time God brings me through, my faith increases.

Your faith will be there to keep you when you can't be there for yourself. Our bodies, which includes our minds, soul, and spirit, is our whole being. Jesus is the Healer of our whole being. Jesus' name is above every name, and it is above Rheumatoid Arthritis, Fibromyalgia, Lupus, Sickle Cell, and all other diseases that cause chronic pain!

We may live with these "Invisible Pain" diseases for the rest of our lives, but every day that we wake up can be another day of Holistic Healing in Jesus' name.

"Now faith is the substance of things hoped for, the evidence of things not seen"

Romans 11:1

We hope by faith that God will heal us even though it might not look like it. We believe by faith that He is able to heal us. God can, and He will heal us. Have FAITH.

Amen

The Importance of Sharing With Family and Friends

When I was first diagnosed with RA, I don't know if it was a matter of pride, embarrassment, or just denial, that I didn't fully share with my family, friends, or my doctor how I was really feeling. I know that when I was in severe pain, they could tell something was wrong. I didn't know how to tell my family and friends that I was in pain every single day. I didn't know how to explain that to them because I didn't fully understand myself.

6My doctors were no help in that department. I'm not saying that they didn't care, but they were so nonchalant when I would tell them about the level of pain, I was in. I've thought about this a lot over the years and I believe that some doctors who specialize in treating Rheumatoid Arthritis and other autoimmune chronic pain diseases are so used to their patients being in pain that they have been desensitized, and so they appear to lack empathy.

Mom Stop Hiding Your Pain

It was so hard telling my two sons I was in pain. I could see the sadness in their eyes. I grew up as a Tomboy, so having sons was great for me. I loved it. We would dance around the house and stay up all night playing video games. Our favorite thing to do was watch wrestling and then practice the moves. I was so active before RA. Instead of telling my sons that I was in pain, I would put forth every effort to try and do everything we use to do. This, of course, would just make me feel even worse. Finally, both my sons expressed their concern for me and said that I should stop trying to hide the pain. Then I started to notice that they were adjusting their lives to accommodate my new life. I will forever be grateful to them for that.

Sharing with my family and close friends was even harder as I began to miss more family functions. I truly hated hearing the doubt in their voices or seeing the suspicious look on their faces when I had to miss an event. The number one issue that causes people to doubt our struggle is there are most often no visible symptoms. Some of my family and friends thought I was using my illness as an excuse not to participate. To combat hat and help my family and friends overcome their doubts and suspicions, I started sharing more about my daily struggle with them. Not directly but indirectly through social media. I would share pictures of my different joints when there was swelling. I also would post every time I was admitted to the hospital.

Understanding Your Family Judgement and Disbelief

I knew I was being judged, and I figured the more informed they were, the less they would judge me. Then I started to hear that people were saying I just wanted attention. I used to get so stressed out about this that it would actually make my illness worst and cause me to have flare-ups. But all that changed once I accepted my diagnosis. I accepted the fact that I am the one who has to deal with this illness every day. I know it's real, and I'm not going to let anyone make me feel ashamed or embarrassed. It didn't matter to me anymore whether they thought I was lying or exaggerating. They needed to come to the same conclusion I had to, and that was I wasn't the same Toni they knew before.

My life had changed, and I believed that if they truly cared about me, they would eventually get there. I had to move on with this disease, just like any other disease. If you are a diabetic, then you know you have to change your diet.

Well, I have RA, and that meant a lifestyle change. I had to stop living behind the mask and start being honest with everyone about how I was feeling physically, mentally, and spiritually. I no longer feel guilty if I can't make a function or event. I have to manage this disease by force, not a choice. I have to put my health first.

Now the people close to me understand that my attendance is tentative depending on the condition of my health at the time. There are times that I push myself even though I may be in pain, and I am blessed to say that my family and friends appreciate it and support me. I am not a complainer. I will share when I am asked about how I am feeling, and I freely share to help encourage others. I believe it's important to help others.

The Importance of Support Groups and Other Resources

It was really important for me to get into some type of support group.

No one else in my immediate or extended family had been diagnosed with RA or Fibromyalgia, and I felt so alone. It's so hard trying to explain something to others that you don't fully understand yourself. Although the people who love me tried to come to some type of understanding, I have come to realize that they will never fully get it because they don't have it.

Join With Other Warriors On The Journey

There are a bunch of support groups out there that you can join online or join a page on Facebook. There are even some in-person support groups. I found these groups using Google. I typed in Rheumatoid Arthritis, Fibromyalgia, and support groups and found some that were on Facebook. They are a really big help. The experience actually motivated me to start my own support group on Facebook called, "RA and Fibromyalgia - Behind The Mask Invisible Pain Support Group." This page I started allows me to promote Holistic Healing as well as share experiences with other believers. It allows me to step outside myself and care for others. It is a constant reminder that I am not alone in this struggle and that there are others who need support and encouragement as well.

It has been a blessing to me to be able to facilitate such a caring and supportive group. Every new member is welcomed with so much love. Everyone is allowed to vent in the safety of our warrior family from all over the globe. We share personal stories and triumphs. We share jokes about our condition that helps us laugh even when we are in pain. Most of all, we share the love of God. A special shout out to all the warriors in our group. You are the absolute best, and I care deeply for each one of you. Smile, you know who you are! Being able to encourage you daily and receive encouragement from you is so valuable to my wellbeing. It's important for me to be able to post the truth about my illness and not have anyone judge me or not believe me. I can say, "Hey, today is not a good day." Then I can tell you all where it hurts and you understand.

It is important for us who are suffering with invisible pain to have support from others outside of our family, outside of our friends, and from outside of our doctors. We don't ever have to meet face to face to have a dialogue with people who are suffering in likeness. We support each other in our struggles and celebrate each other's victories and life events. Being a member of a good support group helps us to come to the realization that although we suffer from illnesses that caused severe chronic pain, life still goes on. We must keep living. Warriors are getting married, having babies, buying houses, and buying cars. It is by God's grace that we press on every day.

How My Testimony Led Me Into Ministry

"And we know that all things work together
for the good to them that love God,
To them who are the called according to his purpose."

Romans 8:28

I have to be truly honest. When I first felt this pain and was diagnosed with RA, I could not see any purpose for what I was going through at all. In the first couple of years, I was in denial. I didn't understand. I asked myself, "What did I do wrong?" and "Why is this happening to me?" I thought I was being punished for something I had done. As I mentioned before, I went through the stages of grief of the old Toni.

However, as I continued on this journey, my faith began to increase. I started to have a different perspective on my illness. I accepted my illness because God had allowed it. No, God did not cause my illness, but because He had allowed it, I had to figure out the purpose. There had to be some good that would come out of this. One of the major changes that I started noticing about myself was that I was beginning to have greater empathy for others, as I mentioned before.

"But as for you, ye thought evil against me,

but God meant unto good"

Genesis 50:20

I took this scripture to heart and began to meditate on it. I knew in my heart that I love God, but I realized that I was walking in my own willful way. The Holy Spirit revealed to me that I was not going to find purpose as long as I was walking in disobedience to God. It was at this point, a couple of years later, in 2019, where God stepped in and began to work on me, in me, and through me. He began to remove people and material things out of my life. This process was very painful. I was gracefully broken. I didn't want to let some people or things go, but in the end, I surrendered my will to God's will.

God's will is the safest place to be. It is in God's will that I now see "purpose." I submit myself to God and His plan for my life. My testimony is God has turned everything around for my good and for the good of His kingdom. I had been writing poems, skits, and plays for over twenty years. I am the director of The LifeLine Evangelistic Drama Ministry at my place of worship, Nebo Christian Ministries, under the leadership of Bishop Larry E Williams and Executive Pastor Dorcas Baker.

In 2017 God revealed to me that He needed me to do more. Something different from what I was already doing. Outside of the church building. I didn't fully understand at that time. However, I proceeded with what I now know was the beginning of a mission. I started a production company with my mom Yvonne and my sister Kiwana. We named it LarMic Productions after my father Larry and my brother Michael who was called home to be with the Lord. We produced a Gospel Stage Play titled "If Thou Would Believe" outside in a park in the inner city of Baltimore, Maryland. I felt that God required me to give back, so the admission was free. It was truly a blessed event. God blessed LarMic Productions, and we were able to produce another Gospel Stage Play titled "Clean This House" in the Fall of the next year 2018.

Although I know that God was blessing the production company, I was struggling in so many areas of my life. Yes, I was wearing an invisible mask. I pretended every day that I was doing fine and that I was happy. I wanted everyone to think I was in control of my life when actually almost every area of my life was out of control. The only time I felt real joy was when I was working on something in my ministries. I knew that was pleasing to God. The stress of trying to hide behind that invisible mask had me in physical pain every day.

In the spring of 2019, the house of cards I had built came tumbling down. God's placed on me, His hands on me, and started to remove everything in my life that was not like Him. I literally lost people, places, and things. God was speaking to me so clearly through the Holy Spirit. And I had to make a choice each time as to whether I was going to refuse to let go and chase after that which God had removed or submit to His will.

After a period of two and a half weeks of crying, struggling to try to negotiate with God, fasting, praying, and submitting all the areas of my life to God and His will, I had a marvelous breakthrough and realized that God allowed me to be crushed so that He could put me back together.

I found that I had a renewed relationship with Christ that was closer than it had ever been. I had fallen in love with Jesus. He had rescued me from me. The call to come outside of the walls of the church became clear. God has purposed for me to reach people who are not coming in the church walls, in the way He has gifted me, through the arts. Beyond The Four Walls Arts Ministry, Behind The Mask Productions, as well as the support group mentioned in an earlier chapter, were birthed from the miraculous encounter with God I experienced.

Taking on the name "The Queen of Trauma Drama" suggested by one of my co-laborers in ministry, I am committed to reaching those who have suffered and are struggling as a result of all types of traumatic experiences. The ministry's mission is to present the gospel of Jesus Christ to everyone we can using the various forms of the Arts and help to guide people on a path to Holistic Healing. To get "Behind The Mask" and heal the mind, body, and spirit.

Moving From Being Fake To Freedom

I'm tired of being fake for goodness sake;

Being fake so I can make everyone around me feel okay.

I'm not okay, and today I just want to be that way;

I want to be free, free to be me, not okay.

Every day my body is riddled with pain;

and I am mentally exhausted and physically drained.

But here comes my fake smile and laugh and I dare not complain;

Because if I do that, I'm made to feel ashamed.

People want to remind me that it could be worst,

And a lot of people have it harder than me;

But isn't that the case for just about everybody?

It sure doesn't change my reality!

As I continue to cope from day to day with my illness;

I've learned one thing that helps me to have less stress.

No matter what anyone says, feel, or how they react;

I trust and believe that God has my back.

He promised to never put more on me then I can bear;

And He keeps His promises because He cares.

My God holds tomorrow in His hand!

I no longer worry about what's to come.

Trusting in God has moved me from being **FAKE to FREEDOM**!

"For I know the thoughts that I think toward you, saith the Lord, thoughts of peace, and not of evil, to give you an expected end."

Jeremiah 29:11

To the families of those who suffer with chronic pain, to the friends, coworkers, and associates. However, you are related to someone who suffers with chronic pain, and I'll leave with you this last statement:

"There is very little that you can physically do to support us who suffer with Chronic Pain Illnesses when we are in pain, what is needed most of all is compassion, understanding, and prayers."

To my mother Yvonne, my two sons Derek and Troy, and all of my family and friends who continue to support me as I travel on this journey, "THANK YOU!"

What's Being Said – The Author & Her Work

"What do I say about this mighty woman of God. I met Toni I guess, about fifteen years ago while working at the American Red Cross. One day we began to share our stories, when I told her about my past being addicted to drugs and alcohol, she almost instantly wrote a stage play. That started our relationship. Toni has written many plays over the years about addicts and about lost souls that have caused many souls to come to Christ and even some to be healed from addiction. She always included an altar call at the end of her plays, and I can't remember one time that we had an empty alter. Toni is truly about saving souls, and even with her medical issues, she pushes pass the pain because souls are at stake. I've seen her do large productions and run around getting everything together and push through even though she was in pain. Then for the next few days, she would be unable to walk, but she still would give God all the glory. Toni, I love you, I am grateful to you, I am grateful for the ministry that God has given you, I am grateful for your love for God, and the love you have for God's people. Continue to be the person that God has called you to be. Love always your sister in Christ."

Betty Johnson, Director
Partners In Action Substance Abuse Ministry
Baltimore, Maryland

"Toni Terry provided excellent instruction for our Knox Presbyterian YouSPEAK youth anti-bullying program. Her use of drama served her well in relating to the students, imparting important values and providing appropriate outlets for self-expression, empathy, and conflict management."

Elder Charese Moore
Knox Presbyterian
Baltimore, Maryland

"Dr. John Burton kindly shared with me the exceptional play that you wrote and that captures so well what doctors need to learn about communicating with and listening to patients. Patients are often our best teachers, a fact that your play richly demonstrates. The Department of Medicine intends to use your play to help teach communication skills to our new interns."

David B. Hellmann, M.D., M.A.C.P
Aliki Perroti Professor of Medicine
Vice Dean, Johns Hopkins Bayview
Johns Hopkins University School of Medicine
Chairman, Department of Medicine
Johns Hopkins Bayview Medical Center

"I had the pleasure of attending one of Toni's Christian plays over ten years ago. I knew immediately that she had an anointing on her life to spread God's word in a unique way. She is insightful, passionate, and filled with what people need to hear and see. It gives me great pleasure to be on the sidelines watching her walk in obedience and using her talent to shine a light on God's word and draw others closer to Him. Her content is relevant, relatable, inspiring, and entertaining. It should not be missed."

Jessie S. Myrick
Pikesville, Maryland

We Invite You To Join Us

Let's continue to connect and be a support to one another. No one knows our pain or struggles but us. Below are links to the Behind The Mask resources. We look forward to connecting with you.

- RA and Fibromyalgia – Behind The Mask Invisible Pain Support Group
  https://www.facebook.com/groups/308127983487067/?ref=share
- Behind The Mask Productions

https://www.facebook.com/queenoftraumadrama19/

- Behindthemaskpro19

https://www.instagram.com/behindthemaskpro19/

- Toni Terry Behind The Mask Tells It All

https://www.youtube.com/channel/UCPJW1RI9Ko3x49ApIAYjFMg

- Website

Behindthemaskproductions.org

- Email
  Queenoftraumadrama19@gmail.com
- Behind The Mask – "Hour of Power" Radio Show

Made in the USA
Monee, IL
04 November 2026

67378023R00036